W9-BLD-623

Play Ukulele Today!

A Complete Guide to the Basics

To access audio visit:
www.halleonard.com/mylibrary
Enter Code
4372-2704-4001-7031

by Barrett Tagliarino

Recording Credits:
Barrett Tagliarino, Ukulele & Narration
Scott Houghton, Vocals
Billy Burke, Engineer

ISBN 978-0-634-07861-3

HAL•LEONARD®
CORPORATION
7777 W. BLUEMOUND RD. P.O. BOX 13819 MILWAUKEE, WI 53213

In Australia Contact:
Hal Leonard Australia Pty. Ltd.
4 Lentara Court
Cheltenham, Victoria, 3192 Australia
Email: ausadmin@halleonard.com

Visit Hal Leonard Online at
www.halleonard.com

Introduction

Track 1

Welcome to *Play Ukulele Today!*—This book is designed to get you started on this fun and easy instrument, with everything you need to know to play chords and melodies, and to learn songs you can sing and play.

About the Audio

The accompanying audio will take you step by step through each lesson and play each example. Much like with a real lesson, the best way to learn this material is to read and practice a while at first on your own, then listen to the audio. With *Play Ukulele Today!*, you can learn at your own pace. If there is ever something that you don't quite understand the first time through, go back to the audio and listen to the track number listed to replay the teacher's explanation. Every musical track has been given its own track number, so if you want to practice a song again, you can find it right away.

On musical examples, the audio has been mixed with the chords on the left channel, and the melody on the right channel. To practice playing chords beneath the melody, turn the balance knob to the right on your stereo (or remove your left headphone). To practice the melody using the track for chord accompaniment only, turn the balance knob to the left. On most single-instrument examples, a metronome or "click track" is used to keep time. The click is often "panned" on the opposite side of the ukulele in the stereo field, so you can practice with as much or as little of the recorded ukulele as you need to hear to help keep your place.

Contents

The Basics

Track 2

The Parts of the Ukulele

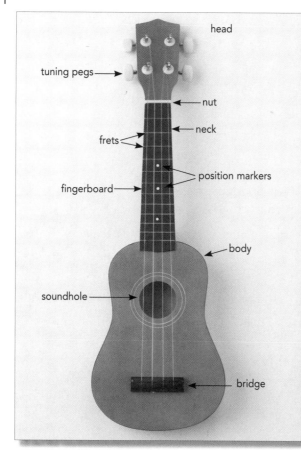

head

tuning pegs →

← nut

← neck

frets →

position markers

fingerboard →

← body

soundhole →

← bridge

Ukuleles come in four sizes: **soprano**, **concert**, **tenor**, and **baritone**.

A **soprano ukulele** is usually about 21 inches long. The **concert** size is about 23 inches and is tuned the same as the soprano. The soprano is most popular and is probably what you have if you're not sure. This book is designed for use with soprano and concert ukuleles and banjo ukuleles.

The **tenor ukulele**, at 26 inches long, is tuned like the soprano and concert except that the fourth string, G, is an octave lower. (Octaves are discussed in the section on music reading.) This book may be applied to the tenor with slight considerations made for the G string.

Baritone ukuleles are the largest at 30 inches and are tuned similarly to the tenor ukulele but a 4th lower. Using this book with a baritone will require *transposition*, especially if you plan to play with other instruments.

How to Hold Your Ukulele

Stand or sit up straight (but not stiff) and support the body of the ukulele with your right forearm. This "arm grip" should be loose enough to allow you to easily strum the strings with your right thumb and fingers. Support the neck at a slight upward angle between your left-hand thumb and first finger. This grip should also be free and easy, to allow your hand to move up or down the neck to any fingerboard position.

Left-handed players may reverse these instructions, as well as restringing and tuning their instruments to be a mirror image of the diagrams. Many lefties decide to go ahead and play right-handed. This is OK—the left (fretting) hand has the most complicated job anyway.

Your Right and Left Hands

Your left-hand fingers are numbered 1 through 4.

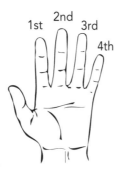

Place the thumb in back of the neck roughly opposite the second finger. Avoid letting your palm touch the back of the neck.

Strum the ukulele in the area where the neck joins the body. This will give the best tone. Don't strum over the sound hole, unless your left hand is playing high up on the neck. In general, strum downward with the thumb and up with the first finger.

Many ukulele players get a nice clear sound by playing with a stiff felt pick. Hold the pick between your crossed thumb and first finger with the point of the pick extending beyond the tip of the first finger.

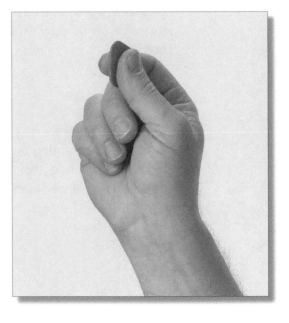

Playing Is Easy

The ukulele strings are numbered 1 to 4, with string number 1 being closest to the floor. That's opposite what you might think—the fourth string is the one closest to your nose.

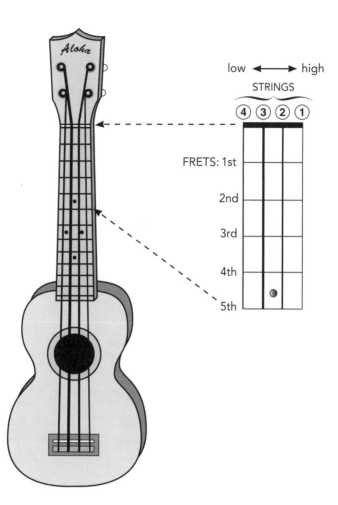

Also notice that fret numbers go up as they get closer to the body of the ukulele. If you play on the higher frets, your hand is said to be moving "up" the neck.

Tuning Up

If you loosen a string by turning its tuning key, the pitch will become lower. If you tighten the string, the pitch will become higher. When two pitches sound exactly the same, they are said to be *in tune*.

Some tuning keys have a small adjustment screw in the end. If your ukulele strings keep going out of tune on you, it's possible this screw may need to be carefully tightened by turning it clockwise. This is a screw you don't want to strip, so just tighten it enough so that the key stays where you put it. If the key is difficult to turn, you may try slightly loosening this screw.

Tuning

Track 5 will play the correct pitch of each string, starting with string number 4. While plucking each string to hear its pitch, carefully adjust the tension to match the pitch on the audio. Higher tension produces higher notes. If you over-tighten the string you may break it; but don't worry, it happens to everyone, and strings are inexpensive.

When a string is too tight, the pitch produced is said to be "sharp." A too-loose string is said to be "flat." The strings of a tuned ukulele produce a little melody:

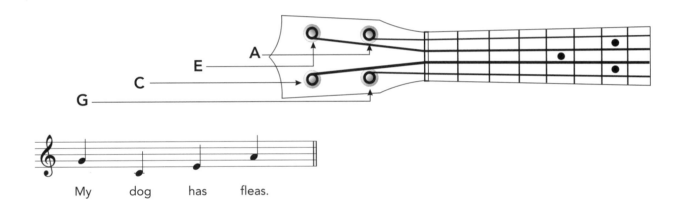

You can also tune to a pitch pipe or an electronic tuner. Both are available at music stores and come with instructions.

Here are a few tips to help get you started:

- Whether tightening or loosening a string, turn the key slowly so that you can concentrate on the changes in pitch. Ukulele notes fade away quickly, so you will need to pluck the string repeatedly to compare it to your tuning reference.

- Instead of tuning a sharp string down to pitch, tune it up. Tuning up allows the string tension to remove the play between the tuning peg gears, which will help the string stay in tune longer. So if you begin with a string that is sharp (too high in pitch), tune it down first (so that it's flat), and then bring it back up to pitch.

Tuning to Other Instruments

Instruments that will be played together should all be tuned to a similar reference. In this age of digital perfection, this is not so hard to achieve anymore, but you may still have to tune to a piano or another instrument that is not at concert pitch.

The ukulele's third string, C, corresponds to middle C on the piano.

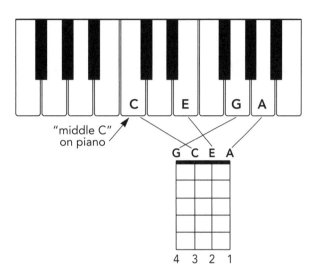

Relative Tuning of the Strings

If you know that one string is correctly tuned, you can use it to tune the others. This method, *relative tuning*, is vital for quickly checking that the ukulele is in tune (at least with itself) at any time. Here's how:

- Let's assume that the third string is correctly tuned to C. You can start with whichever string you think is closest to being in tune once you understand the system. We'll start with C because it's the lowest available note on the ukulele.

- Press the third string at the seventh fret. This is the pitch G, to which you tune the open (unfretted) fourth string. Play the two notes together and adjust the fourth string until the two strings match.

- Now press the third string at the fourth fret. This is the pitch E, to which you tune your open second string. Play the two notes together, adjusting the open second string until it matches the fretted note on the third string.

- Finally, press the second string at the fifth fret. The open first string, A, should be tuned to match this note.

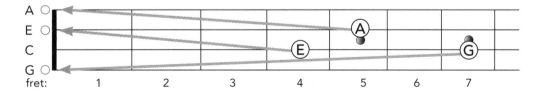

Track 5

Tuning Notes

How to Read Music

Track 6

Pitch

Music is written in **notes** on a **staff**. The staff has five lines with four spaces between them. Where a note is written on the staff determines its **pitch** (highness or lowness).

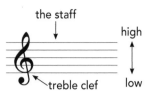

At the beginning of the staff is a **clef sign**. Most melodies are written in the **treble clef**.

Each line and space of the staff has a letter name. The lines are (from bottom to top) **E–G–B–D–F**, which you can remember as **E**very **G**ood **B**oy **D**oes **F**ine. The spaces are (from bottom to top) **F–A–C–E**, which spells "**Face**."

The lines and spaces together spell the **musical alphabet** using the first seven letters of the English alphabet, A through G. Once G is reached, the musical alphabet starts over. Two different notes with the same letter name—for instance, E on the first line and E on the fourth space—are said to be an **octave** (eight notes) apart.

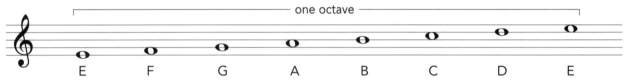

Rhythm

The staff is divided into several parts by **bar lines**. The space between two bar lines is called a **measure** (also known as a "bar"). To end a piece of music, a **double bar line** is placed on the staff.

Each measure contains a group of **beats**. Beats are the steady pulse of music. You respond to the pulse or beat when you tap your foot. The **time signature** tells you how many beats are in a measure.

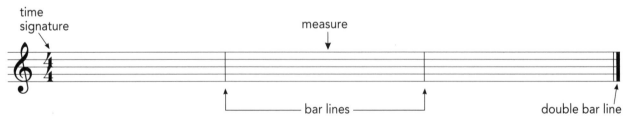

Notes indicate the length (number of counts) of musical sound.

You can tell which pitch to play by the position of a note on the staff and how to long to play it by its shape.

Track 7

Lesson 2 Playing Chords

The ukulele's role is most often to play *chords*, which provide accompaniment for singing or another instrument carrying the melody. Chords consist of two or more notes strummed at the same time. In fact, most ukulele chords use all four strings, making the "uke" easy and fun to play.

To play a chord, first get your left-hand fingers into position. The dots on each grid tell you where to fret the strings, and the numbers tell you which fingers to use. Depress the strings with the tips of your fingers, and arch your fingers to avoid touching strings that are to be played open. Strum the strings with a downward motion of your thumb or pick. All strings should sound as one—not separately.

C

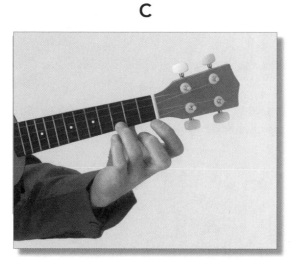

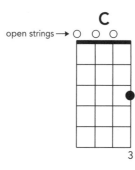

G7

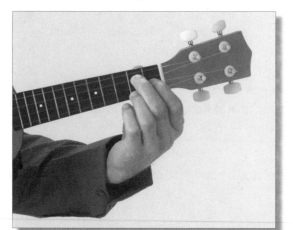

► Keep your left-hand fingernails trimmed for easier fretting.

Slash Rhythms

Chord symbols are written above the staff, and *slash rhythms* show when the chords are strummed and how long to let them ring. Slash rhythms cover the middle two spaces of the staff to let you know chords are to be played instead of single notes. No clef sign is necessary when writing slash rhythms, since they don't indicate pitch.

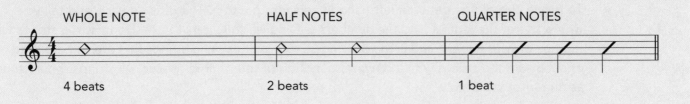

WHOLE NOTE	HALF NOTES	QUARTER NOTES
4 beats	2 beats	1 beat

Often simple slash marks with no stems are used, which tells you to "play time" in the style of the piece. For the ukulele, we can usually interpret this to mean the same as the quarter-note slash rhythm: four strums per measure.

Practice the following exercise strumming once for each slash mark, using downstrokes only. Keep a steady beat, and change chord fingerings as quickly as you can.

C-G7

Track 8

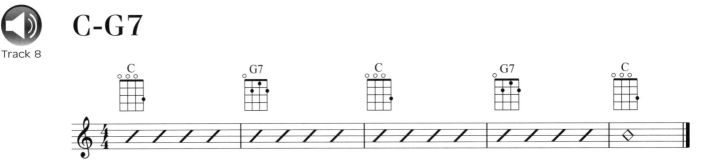

As you practice the transition between these chords, you may notice that there's no need to lift the third finger off the fretboard. That's a good thing! Keep the third finger down and just *slide* it from the third to the second fret when going from C to G7. Then slide the third finger back up to the third fret when changing from G7 to C.

Now apply the same "quarter-note strum" to the song below, playing along with the audio.

Strum-a-Thon

Track 9

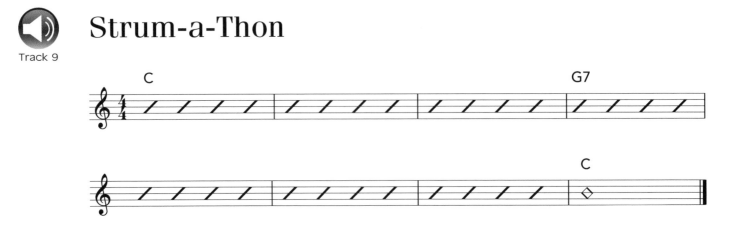

Now let's add two more chords to your repertoire: G and D7.

G

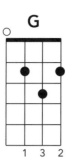

D7

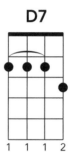

The D7 is our first *barre* chord. For barre chords, your finger must flatten out across multiple strings. All the strings should be pressed into solid contact with the fret to make a clear sound when you strum the chord. For this particular chord, the first string is also played by the second finger, one fret higher than the first, so it doesn't matter if your barre covers the first string.

Don't give up if you can't play the barre chord at first—practice makes perfect. Just try your best, and let your fingers adapt to the new position over time.

Step Up to the Barre

Track 10

► As you're learning new chords, pluck each string of the chord individually to make sure the notes are fretted properly.

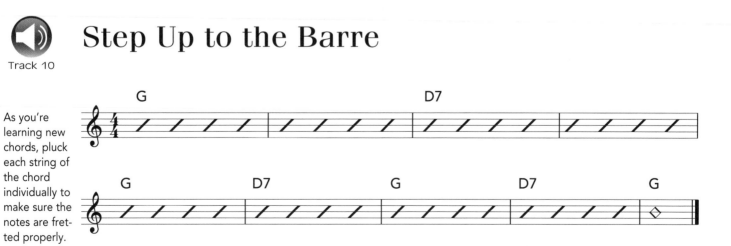

Keeping Time

Having trouble keeping a steady rhythm? Tap your foot and count out loud. Each time the foot comes down marks one beat. In 4/4 time, tap your foot four times in each measure, and count "1, 2, 3, 4." The first beat of each new measure should be accented slightly—this is indicated below by the symbol ">."

Review the fingering for the C chord and then practice this exercise until you can play it well.

Track 11

Chord Study

Tracks 12–14 use the four chords you have learned so far. The chords are arranged in sequences called *chord progressions*.

Track 12

Progression 1

Now try switching between these chords in different sequences and rhythms.

Track 13

Progression 2

Track 14

Progression 3

Two New Chords: F and A

F

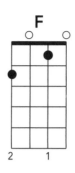

A

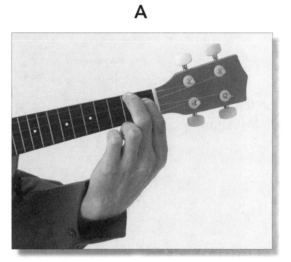

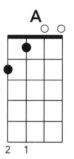

Barbershop

► Remember to arch your fingers to allow the open strings of a chord to ring out properly.

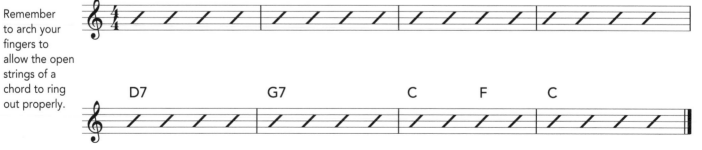

Notes on the First String: A

In addition to chords, you can also play melodies on the ukulele by using one string at a time. Start by playing all downstrokes with the thumb or pick. Later we'll add upstrokes with the first finger or pick. Use whichever you prefer; you may find the pick gives a cleaner sound, especially when playing upstrokes.

A

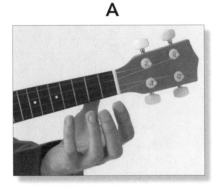

■ Your first note, A, is an "open-string" tone. There's nothing to fret—simply pluck (or pick) the open first string.

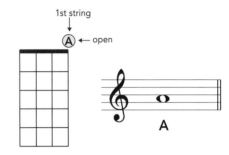

B

■ For the next note, B, place your second finger on the second fret of the first string and pluck.

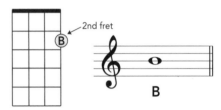

C

► Remember, your finger belongs directly behind the metal fret. If you place it on top of the fret, or too far back, you'll have difficulty getting a clear sound.

■ To play C, place your third finger on the third fret and pluck the first string.

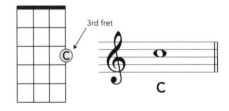

Learn to recognize these notes both on the fretboard and on the staff. Then, when you're comfortable playing the notes individually, try this short exercise. Speak the note names aloud as you play (e.g., "A, B, C, B...").

Track 18

A-B-C

► Be sure to play the full note durations as shown in the music notation; don't cut off notes from ringing too early.

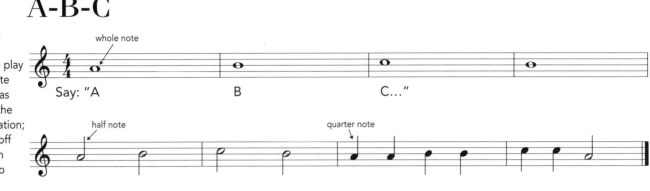

Say: "A   B   C..."

Of course, the best way to really learn these notes is to use them in some tunes. Start slowly with the following melodies, and keep your pace nice and even.

Track 19

First Melody

Steady rhythm when playing single notes is just as important as when playing chords. Again, tap your foot on each beat and count along with all four beats in each measure.

Track 20

Second Melody

Third Melody

Track 21

► It's also good practice to read through each song without your ukulele first: tap the beat with your foot, count aloud, and clap through the rhythms.

Sharps, Flats, and Naturals

Sharps and flats are part of a group of musical symbols called *accidentals*, which raise or lower the pitch of a note:

A *sharp* (♯) raises the pitch of a note by one fret.

A *flat* (♭) lowers the pitch of a note by one fret.

A *natural* (♮) cancels a previous sharp or flat, returning a note to its original pitch.

In musical terms, the distance of one fret is called a *half step*. When a song requires a note to be a half step higher or lower, you'll see a sharp (♯), flat (♭), or natural (♮) sign in front of it.

Track 22

Two New Notes: B♭ and C♯

These are notes named with *accidentals*, between the natural notes we've already learned.

B♭

► This is one fret *lower* than the B note you already learned.

■ For the note B-flat (B♭), place your first finger on the first fret and pluck the first string.

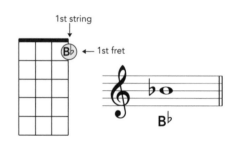

C♯

► This is one fret *higher* than the C note you already learned.

■ To play C-sharp (C♯), place your fourth finger on the fourth fret and pluck the first string.

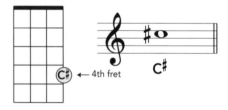

Accidentals apply only throughout the measure in which they appear. An accidental must be restated if the melody uses it again in a later measure.

Track 23

B♭-C♯

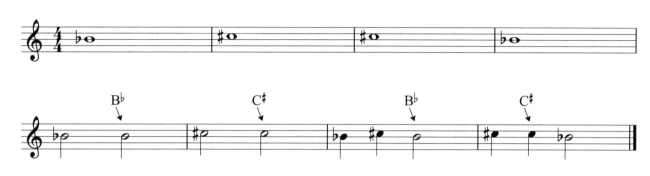

Here is a tune to practice all five notes we've learned so far. Don't be afraid to review the A, B, and C notes again before tackling this one!

Track 24

Play It!

► Watch out for the natural sign!

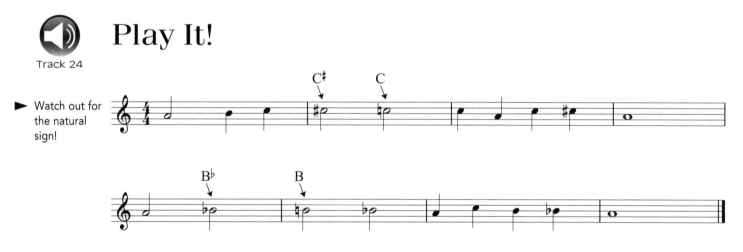

Notes on the Second String: E

Your next three notes are all played on the second string, E. You might want to check your tuning on that string before going any farther.

E

■ To play the note E, just pluck the open second string.

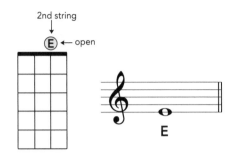

F

■ To play the note F, place your first finger on the first fret of the second string.

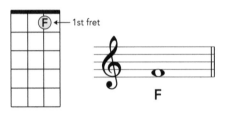

G

■ To play the note G, place your third finger on the third fret of the second string.

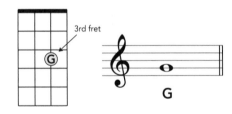

Second-String Study

Track 26

Here's a single-note melody that uses notes we have learned on the first and second strings.

Naturals

Track 27

Two New Notes: F♯ and A♭

F♯

► This is one fret *higher* than the F note you already learned.

■ To play the note F♯, place your second finger on the second fret of the second string.

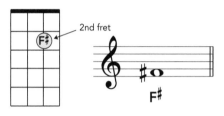

A♭

► This is one fret *higher* than the G note you already learned.

■ To play the note A♭, place your fourth finger on the fourth fret of the second string.

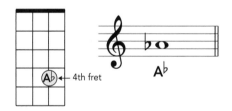

While as a rule accidentals only apply to the measure in which they appear, sometimes the music will have a ***courtesy accidental*** just to remind you what the correct note is.

Accidentals

Track 28

Enharmonic Equivalents

The next song has a "new" note, G♯. G♯ is really a note you already know as A♭. How can one note have two names? It just depends on which way you approach it: up from G or down from A. Notes like G♯ and A♭ are called *enharmonic equivalents*—a fancy way of saying "two names for the same pitch."

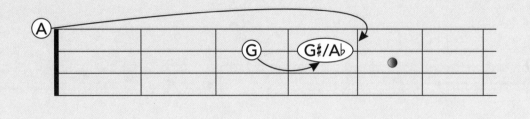

Gee, My New Friend Is Sharp

Track 29

You can read and play a written vocal melody on the ukulele. When the melody becomes familiar (or if it's one you already know), sing it while you strum the chords.

Mary Had a Little Lamb

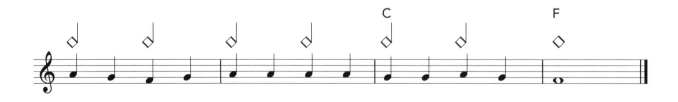

Notes on the Third String: C

Track 30

Your next two notes are played on the third string, C. The third string will be the last string we'll use to read single notes on soprano and concert ukuleles.

Our new notes on the third string are below the range of the staff in treble clef. If a note is too low or high to fit on the lines or spaces of the staff, we use *ledger lines*, which extend the staff downward or upward.

C

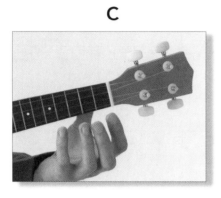

■ To play the note C, just pluck the open third string.

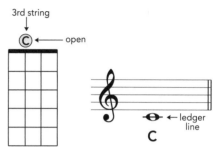

D

■ To play the note D, place your second finger on the second fret of the third string.

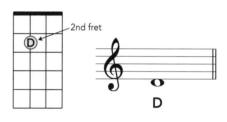

Practice reading the two new notes.

C-D

Here is an exercise that uses the natural notes we've learned on the top three strings.

All Natural

Track 31

Accidentals on the Third String: C♯ and E♭

C♯ (D♭)

■ To play the note C♯ (or its enharmonic equivalent, D♭), place your first finger on the first fret of the third string.

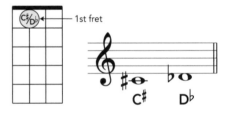

1st fret

C♯   D♭

D♯ (E♭)

■ To play the note E♭ (or its enharmonic equivalent, D♯), place your third finger on the third fret of the third string.

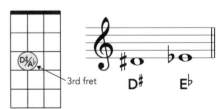

3rd fret

D♯   E♭

Reading Rhythms

Track 32

Introducing Rests

In addition to notes, songs may also contain silences, or *rests*—beats in which you play or sing nothing at all. A rest is a musical pause. Rests are like notes in that they have their own rhythmic values, instructing you how long (or for how many beats) to pause:

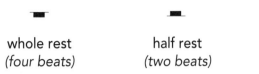

whole rest
(four beats)

half rest
(two beats)

quarter rest
(one beat)

You should stop any previous notes or chords from ringing during a rest. To do this, you will need to use *string damping:*

- After a note or chord, decrease the pressure of your fretting-hand finger(s) on the strings—but don't let go of the neck completely. Let your fretting-hand fingers *damp* (lightly touch) all the strings to stop their vibrations.
- You can also play a rest by damping all the strings with the palm of your strumming hand.

Play the chords shown.

Track 33

Slash Rhythms With Rests

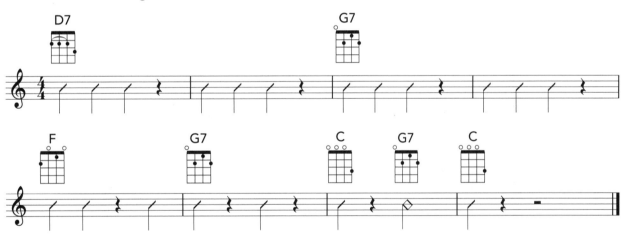

Track 34

Single-Note Melody With Rests

► Try to look a little ahead as you play.

Introducing Eighth Notes

If you divide a quarter note in half, what you get is an *eighth note*. An eighth note looks like a quarter note, but with a flag on its stem.

Two eighth notes equal one quarter note. To help you keep track of the beat, consecutive eighth notes are connected with a beam instead of having flags.

To count eighth notes, divide the beat into two, and use "and" between the beats. Practice this first by counting aloud while tapping your foot on the beat, and then by playing the notes while counting and tapping.

Track 35

Eighth rests are counted the same way, but you pause instead of playing.

Alternating Downstrokes and Upstrokes

For any measure where you strum chords using eighth-note rhythms, alternate between strumming down with your thumb on the beat and up with your index finger on the "and." This is a little tricky at first, so go super slow.

If you are using a pick to strum the chords, the same principle of alternating up and downstrokes applies.

Track 36

Eighth-Note Rhythm

► Keep your hand moving up and down with your foot even when you are just waiting to play a note. It helps you stay in time.

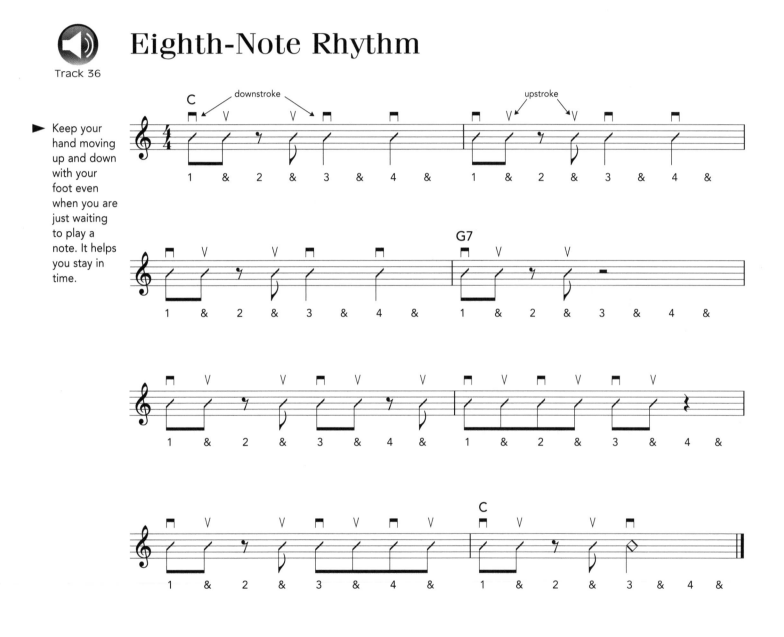

Minor Chords

When a chord was named with only a letter, it was really just short for a name such as *F major* or *F maj*. Now we have some *minor chords*, which must always have *m* in the symbol.

Cm

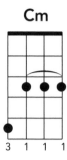

Cm

3 1 1 1

Em

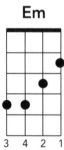

Em

3 4 2 1

Let's try out these minor chords in some familiar music. First play the simple melody of "Joshua Fought the Battle of Jericho," then strum the chords in steady quarter notes. This melody includes a note we haven't played before—E♭ on the third fret of the third string.

Joshua Fought the Battle of Jericho

Repeat signs () tell you to repeat everything in between them. If only one sign appears (:‖), repeat from the beginning of the piece.

Doo-Wop

Track 39

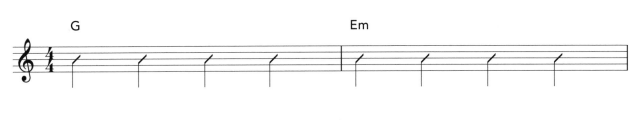

repeat from the beginning

3/4 Time

Track 40

The next song is in ***3/4*** meter. This means there are three beats (quarter notes) per measure.

3/4 time feels very different from 4/4 time. A song in 3/4 is often called a ***waltz***. Be sure to accent the first beat of each measure just slightly; this will help you feel the new meter.

Introducing the Pickup

Instead of starting a song with a rest, a *pickup measure* may be used. A pickup measure is an incomplete measure that deletes any opening rests. So, if a pickup to a song in 4/4 has only one beat, you count "1, 2, 3," and start playing on beat 4.

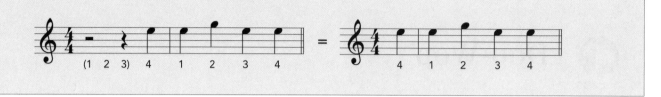

"Clementine" is a waltz that includes a new (but easy) chord for us, C7. Notice the pickup measure: the melody begins on beat 3. The first chord starts on beat 1. Chord diagrams are included to show the new chord, C7, and to refresh your memory of F and C.

Practice the chords until you can strum throughout the whole song without stopping. Then play the melody on your ukulele. Finally, strum the chords while singing the song.

Track 41

Clementine

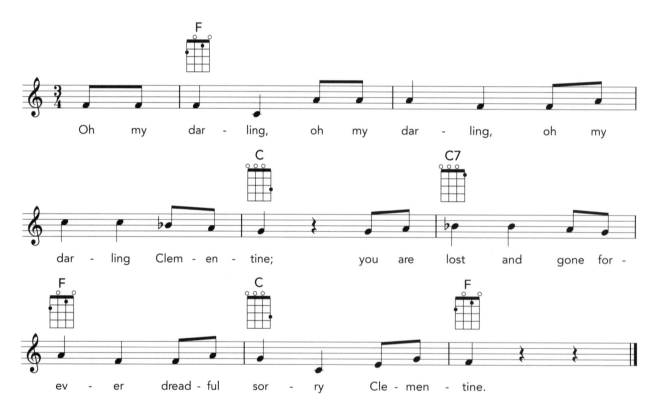

Ties and Dots

The *tie* is a curved line that connects two notes of the same pitch. When you see a tie, play the first note and then hold it for the total value of both notes.

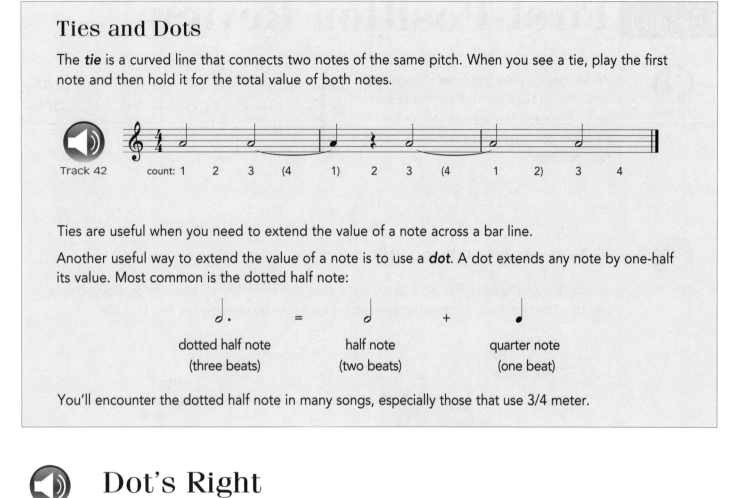

Track 42   count: 1 2 3 (4 1) 2 3 (4 1 2) 3 4

Ties are useful when you need to extend the value of a note across a bar line.

Another useful way to extend the value of a note is to use a *dot*. A dot extends any note by one-half its value. Most common is the dotted half note:

       dotted half note   =   half note   +   quarter note

       (three beats)   (two beats)   (one beat)

You'll encounter the dotted half note in many songs, especially those that use 3/4 meter.

Dot's Right

Track 43

First-Position Review

Track 44

We've covered the top three strings, but let's double back and review the notes we've learned. This area of the neck—from the open strings to fret 4—is called *first position*.

A	A#/Bb	B	C	C#/Db
E	F	F#/Gb	G	G#/Ab
C	C#/Db	D	D#/Eb	E
G				

Track 45

A New Barre Chord: B♭

To play the B♭ major chord, we'll use a first-finger barre on the top two strings. Keep the second and third fingers arched, while flattening the first finger by relaxing the last knuckle.

Bb

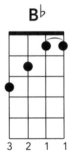

Bb

3 2 1 1

Notice the similarity in the shape of the B♭ chord to A when you play this exercise.

Track 46

It's Fab!

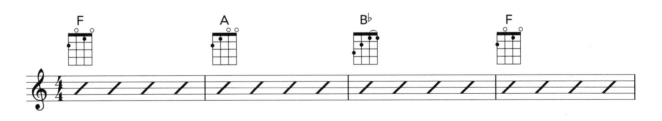

Notes at the Fifth Fret

Although the ukulele is so small you can reach notes on the fifth fret by slightly stretching, it's easier to keep your place by following the "one finger per fret" rule. If you move your first finger to the second fret, your left hand is now said to be in *second position*, and the notes at the fifth fret will be played with your fourth finger.

D

▶ Remember to anchor your thumb on the back of the neck roughly the opposite of your middle finger.

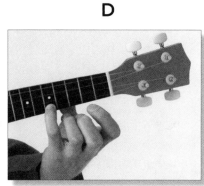

■ To play the high D note, place your fourth finger at the fifth fret of the first string.

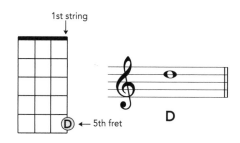

A

■ To play the A note, place your fourth finger at the fifth fret of the second string.

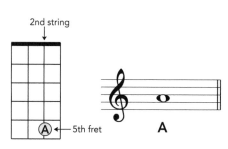

F

■ To play the F note, place your fourth finger at the fifth fret of the third string.

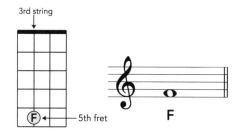

Let's use the notes we just learned to play "Amazing Grace." Keep your first finger on the second fret; however, for smoothness, use the fourth finger for the A note and the *third* finger for the F note on the fifth fret.

Remember to count three beats for each measure, starting the melody on beat 3 of the pickup measure. Then practice the chords, counting each measure of 3/4 time aloud. Finally, strum the chords in quarter notes, and sing the lyrics to this classic song.

Amazing Grace

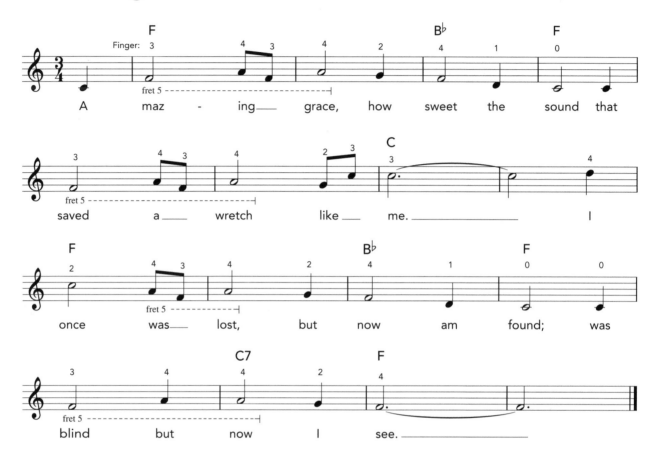

There's More Than One Place to Find a Note

The lowest notes we can play, on frets 0 (open) through 3 of the third string, are only available in first position. But the other notes we've learned may also be found higher up the neck on lower strings.

For instance, the note E, which we learned as the open second string, may also be fretted at the fourth fret of the third string. Also, we now have two places to play F and A.

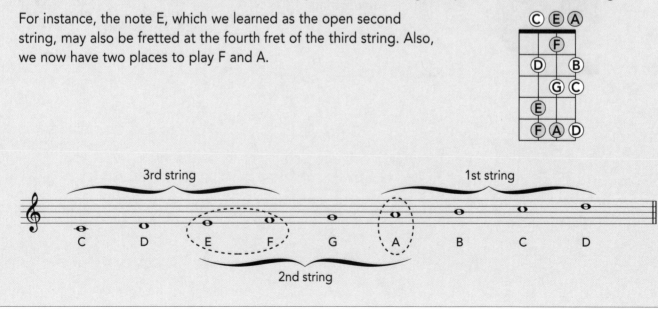

Jumping Octaves

Much of the ukulele's appeal stems from its very high range of notes. But we only have three strings on which to read melodies, which is less than most stringed instruments. As a result, sometimes it's necessary to play notes an *octave* (eight notes) higher or lower than written when reading, then remember to switch them back when singing.

Here's an example. "Shalom Chaverim" starts on B *below the staff*, which is lower than we can play. But that doesn't mean we can't learn the song! We'll read the B an octave higher, on the second fret of the first string. Let's also drop the high E in measure 3 down by an octave, playing it on the open second string.

Shalom Chaverim

Major Scales

Track 49

Now it's time to start learning about scales. "What's a scale?" you ask. A **scale** is an arrangement of notes in a specific, sequential pattern. Most scales use eight notes, with the top and bottom notes being an octave apart.

Two things give a scale its name: its lowest note (called the root), and the pattern of whole and half steps it uses. (A **whole step** is two frets; a **half step** is one fret.)

A **major** scale is always built using this interval formula:

whole – whole – half – whole – whole – whole – half

Let's take a look at some major scales!

► Notice that in a C major scale, there are only natural notes: no sharps or flats.

The C Major Scale

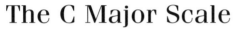

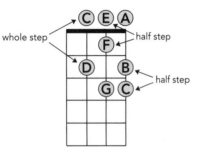

► Notice that in a D major scale, there are two sharps: F♯ and C♯.

The D Major Scale

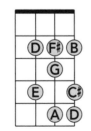

Movable Major Scale Forms

Track 50

Any scale pattern that does not use open strings can be used all over the neck to play scales from different roots. For instance, just find the desired root note on string 3 or 2, then apply one of the patterns below—and there's your scale.

Root on the Third String

► The circled dots in the diagram represent the root note of the major scale form.

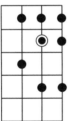

Root on the Second String

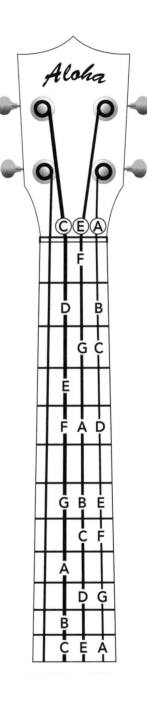

With moveable scale forms we can start on any of the twelve possible roots. Let's do just that to play some major scales. We can play an F major scale in fifth position, starting with the root on the third string, fifth fret. The highest note will be F on the eighth fret of the first string.

Track 51

The F Major Scale

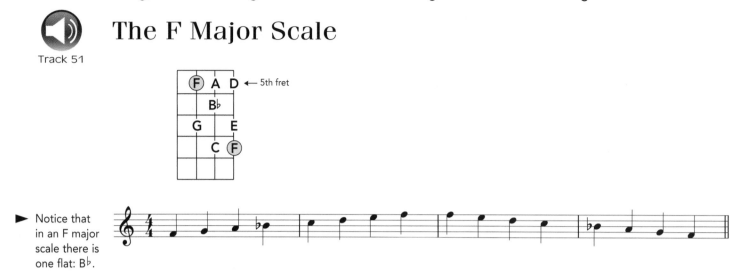

← 5th fret

► Notice that in an F major scale there is one flat: B♭.

We can play an A major scale in fourth position, starting with the second finger on the second string, fifth fret. The highest note in the fingering pattern is E on the seventh fret of the first string. When practicing a pattern like this one (where there are notes included below the root), start on the root, play to the highest note, and then descend to the lowest note. Then climb back up and finish the scale on the root to help reinforce its sound to your ear.

Remember to start with the second (middle) finger.

Track 52

The A Major Scale

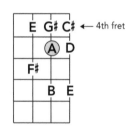

← 4th fret

► Notice that in an A major scale there are three sharps: F♯, C♯, and G♯.

Key Signatures

In written music, a **key signature** is found at the beginning of the staff, between the clef and the time signature. It defines what notes will be sharp or flat—or essentially, what key you'll be playing in.

key signature

Key of E, four sharps

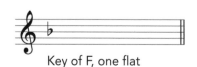

Key of F, one flat

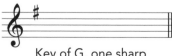

Key of G, one sharp

So What's a Key?

Good question. **Key** and **scale** are almost the same thing. When we know a scale—like E major—we have all the notes we need to play in the corresponding key—E major!

Keys have two components in common with scales:

1) A root, or **tonic**, which is the defining note. This is often (but not always) the first or last note in a piece of music, and it usually feels the most resolved, or "at rest."

2) A **quality**. In this case, a major scale corresponds to a major key.

Track 53

G's the Key

► Watch the key signature; it tells you what notes to play sharp (or flat) throughout the song.

Track 54

Red River Valley

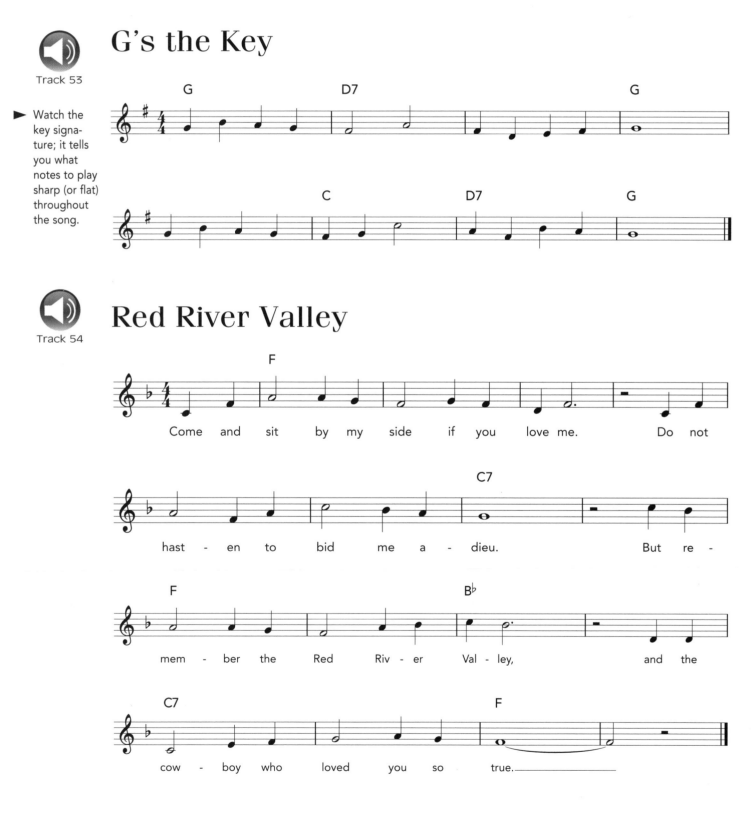

Come and sit by my side if you love me. Do not hast - en to bid me a - dieu. But re - mem - ber the Red Riv - er Val - ley, and the cow - boy who loved you so true.

Home on the Range

Minor Scales

Track 56

We've checked out some major scales. A minor scale has a different interval formula:

whole – half – whole – whole – half – whole – whole

Let's look at some minor scales on the staff and the ukulele fingerboard.

C Minor

Track 57

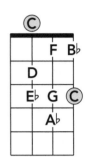

► Notice that in a C minor scale there are three flats: B♭, E♭, and A♭.

D Minor

Track 58

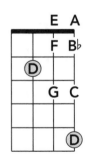

► Notice that in a D minor scale there is only one flat: B♭.

Movable Minor Scale Forms

These shapes produce a minor scale from whichever root they're started on. Again, locate the desired root, and voilà!—as if by magic, a minor scale in any key you need.

Root on the Third String

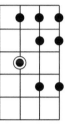

Root on the Second String

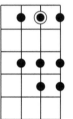

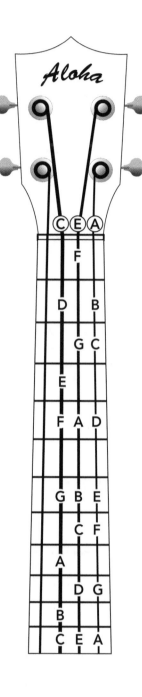

Major vs. Minor

The difference between major and minor scales is not just about whole and half steps—it's about how they *sound*. Take a minute to compare a major and a minor scale—like C major and C minor. Notice how each makes you feel? It's difficult to put into words, but generally we say that major scales (and keys) have a strong, upbeat, or happy quality, while minor scales and keys have a darker, sadder quality.

Track 59

E Minor Tragedy

Track 60

G Minor Blues

Two New Chords: Dm and Am

Our next tune features two minor chords, Dm and Am. Let's practice these new chords first.

Dm

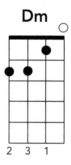

Am

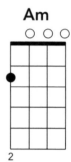

Drunken Sailor

Track 61

What shall we do with the drunk-en sail-or,

what shall we do with the drunk-en sail-or, what shall we do with the

drunk-en sail-or, ear-ly in the morn-ing?

Chord Glossary

These are chords you will find in many popular songs. You don't have to buy music that is written specifically for the ukulele—just make sure the music has chord symbols.

A good way to learn new songs and chords at the same time is to draw ukulele chord diagrams directly above the chord symbols on the music. You'll be surprised by how quickly you learn new chords when you copy the diagrams this way.

Major Chords

A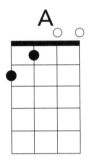

A♯ / B♭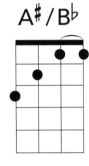

B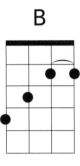

C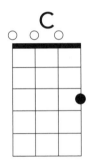

C♯ / D♭

D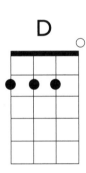

D♯ / E♭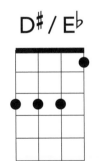

E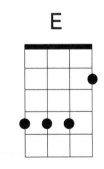

F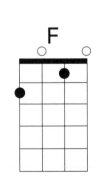

F♯ / G♭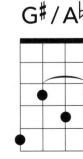

G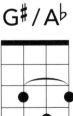

G♯ / A♭

Minor Chords

Am
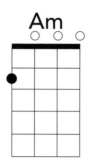

A#m/B♭m
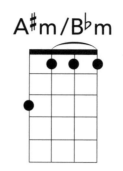

Bm

Cm
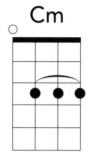

C#m/D♭m
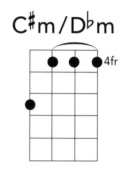

Dm
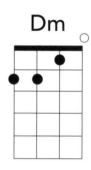

D#m/E♭m
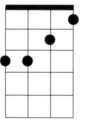

Em
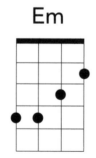

Fm
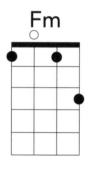

F#m/G♭m
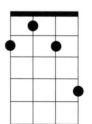

Gm
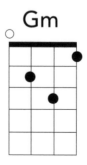

G#m/A♭m
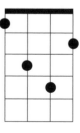

Dominant Chords

A7
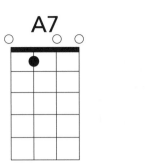

A#7/B♭7
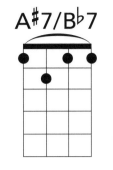

B7
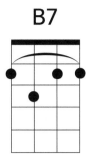

C7
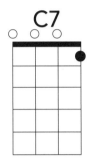

C#7/D♭7

D7

D#7/E♭7
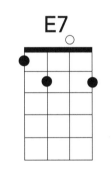

E7

F7

F#7/G♭7
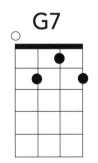

G7
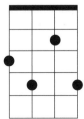

G#7/A♭7
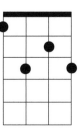

Miscellaneous Moveable Chord Forms

Circled note = root

C6

D6

A°7
E♭°7
F#°7
C°7

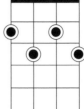

A♭°7
D°7
F°7
B°7

Cmaj7

Dmaj7

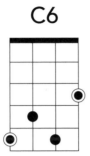
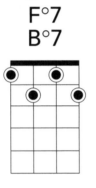
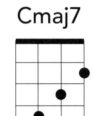
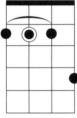

Cm7

Dm7

Dm7♭5

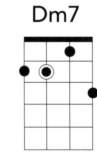

Am7♭5

D+

B♭+

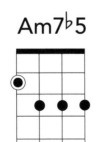
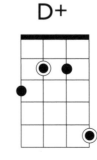
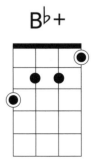

How to Change a String

Strings need to be changed when they break, or when they get old and go "dead" in tone. It's easiest to remove and replace one string at a time. Make sure to replace with the same gauge of each string. Wrap one end of the new string through the bridge hole as shown in the diagram and pull it tight. Then feed the other end through the tuning peg hole, making sure the string sits in the nut slot and is not hung up on the edge of the fingerboard. Leave about a half inch of slack, to allow the string to wrap around the tuning post about three times when tightened. Hold it in place with one hand while tightening until it stays by itself. Trim off the excess string at the top and bottom with a pair of wire cutters, and then tune the string up to pitch.

1. Insert string through bridge hole from the top.

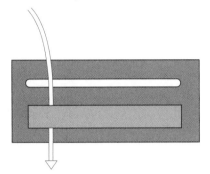

2. Wrap over block, under string, through loop.

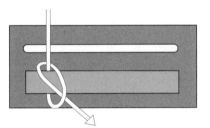

3. Wrap until last winding is near bottom hole.

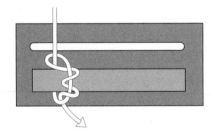

4. Pull to tighten.

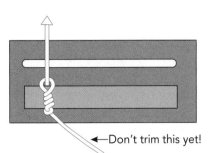

←Don't trim this yet!

5. Insert string into peg from the inside of the headstock.

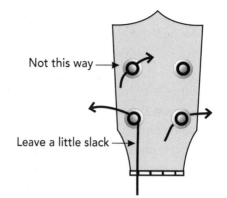

Not this way

Leave a little slack

6. Pinch the string on the peg for several turns to keep the string from slipping.

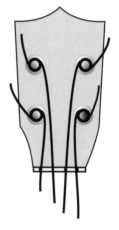

7. Turn tuning key with your other hand. Make sure the string wraps neatly down the peg. Tune string to pitch and make sure it isn't slipping.

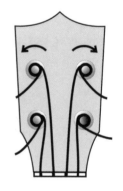

8. Trim off excess string at both ends of the ukulele, but leave about 1/4".

New strings will go through a stretching period before they stay in tune. You can tug on them a little bit to speed up the process. Tune up regularly as you play. If you are sure you have the strings installed correctly and the ukulele still won't stay in tune, you may have loose tuning pegs. Most guitar shops can fix this and other problems.